Krzysztof Siwczyk

A Calligraphy of Days

SELECTED POEMS

TRANSLATED BY PIOTR FLORCZYK
AND ALICE-CATHERINE CARLS

Seagull
BOOKS

LONDON NEW YORK CALCUTTA

Seagull Books, 2024

Text © Krzysztof Siwczyk, 2024

First published in English translation by Seagull Books, 2024
English translation and Afterword © Piotr Florczyk
and Alice-Catherine Carls, 2024

ISBN 978 1 8030 9 418 2

British Library Cataloguing-in-Publication Data
A catalogue record for this book is available from the British Library

Typeset by Seagull Books, Calcutta, India
Printed and bound by WordsWorth India, New Delhi, India

contents

PART I

Finger Drawing + 3

My Youthful Narcissism + 4

Do Not Take the Girl to Christ + 6

Poem for Anne Sexton + 7

For + 9

Wild Kids + 10

In Three Sentences + 12

The Template + 13

* * * + 14

* * * + 15

* * * + 16

People You Know + 17

The North Sea + 18

In Broad Daylight + 20

Transitions + 21

What Next + 22

Sleepy Prewar + 23

Florida + 24

This Rather Than That + 25

Of Course + 26

Skills + 27

Boundaries + 28

The Attempt + 30

A List of Essential Practices + 31

PART II

Crematoria I   ✦   35

Spittoon   ✦   36

Bathing   ✦   37

Patience   ✦   38

After (Confessional Poetry)   ✦   39

Meanwhile   ✦   40

Impersonal   ✦   41

Travellers   ✦   42

Philately   ✦   43

Results   ✦   44

Painting and Imaging   ✦   45

Changes   ✦   46

The Numismatist   ✦   47

Accidental Hope   ✦   48

On Your Way Out   ✦   49

PART III

[The Generous Street of Souvenirs]   ✦   53

March Report   ✦   54

Docklands   ✦   55

Bare Facts   ✦   56

[Entering the Dwellings of Sad Religions]   ✦   57

Depth   ✦   58

Outside the Window   ✦   59

* * *   ✦   60

The City • 61

From Afar • 62

False Bottom • 63

From a Diary • 64

Rose • 65

Particulars and Ideas • 66

So • 67

Finally • 68

[A Merciful Amnesia Manages Current Affairs] • 69

First Impression • 70

* * * • 71

April Fools' Day • 72

Belief System • 73

A Way of Life • 74

Settling Scores • 75

A New Novel • 76

The Speaker • 77

Translators' Afterword • 78

Translators' Acknowledgements • 82

PART I

Finger Drawing

On the table between a key and a Maggi cube
she painted God with powdered sugar
just for herself
I walked into the kitchen She quietly
blew God off the table
onto the polished linoleum
and gave me her fingers to lick
My eyelids closed immediately
like a power lock and I felt in my mouth
His body and taste

My Youthful Narcissism

My youthful narcissism went off the rails this year
I'm already a big old boy
I don't watch porn or ride a mountain bike
I prefer to visit an old lady
to drink raspberry tea and eat cheesecake with her

We talk about whether it is still worth
replacing the old bathtub with a new one
Will they bring coal from the depot for the winter
and who will shovel it into the basement
We also look at her grandkids' holiday postcards

We hug for a friendly goodbye
Fretting—to leave a good impression—
I'm not sure if I'll manage to land my kiss
on the suede pillow of an old cheek

I'm going home sure that I've
embraced the very spectre of Time
and that it will be a few years
before I replace my yellowed old
bathtub

Only my buddies in tank tops
fresh pink nipples shining through
say that I'm a pussy
who shouldn't hang out with that old hag

Do Not Take the Girl to Christ

Noon A department store packed to the brim
like a snake that swallowed a small rabbit
It's noisy A house-slipper salesman stands
by the entrance door and rubs his hands
I stare I begin to look in my hands' creases
for the bit of warmth they took away
from a girl's silky shoulder blades yesterday
I remember the hands that carried in their lines
that stolen heat to the crucified Christ
in the narthex of an ugly church
The transparent space between His ribs
spoke all the tenderness I remembered
Suddenly my hands chilled by
the wood and the skin-coloured paint
forgot the girl's warmth Suddenly
Noon A department store packed to the brim
A house-slipper salesman is closing shop
I have found my empty hands

Poem for Anne Sexton

I hate you Anne Sexton
Our breakfast was not consummated
First we were supposed to feed
my rodent with fresh grass
Later, chase French cognac
with marzipan bars from Wedel
Strip naked
Cut off the sky with one long
Wink of the eye and
kiss the larvae of our slippery lips
I hate you Anne Sexton

Our breakfast was not consummated
Already undressed we were supposed to
roll around in peanut butter and
lick it off with our tongues

Our breakfast was not consummated
God was not an embarrassed brat
watching our naked frolics

Surely by now as calm
as a blank slide photo
you scurry through His hands
in the shower of some vile motel

I'm wildly jealous of Him

For

      M.

Like your old pope, I too
know how to ski Have fresh breath and
can reshape with open hands
your faded calves the colour of white wine
into a madness of shards the colour of (true) blood
how good they must taste under your thin skin

Like your God, I too can
be silent I will even be more silent in the morning
when we wake up on a narrow love-seat and you
pull out of my eye a lash you lost in the night
and wash my red face with a tonic For you
I can impersonate God perfectly Nothing

more

Wild Kids

Autumn in the church The heat isn't on yet It's cold
I am standing before a mud-coloured cross
Polished to a shine by a million touches
Christ's feet as cold as the handrails
of morning buses

Two kids enter the church rubbing together
Styrofoam they found by a furniture store
Finish eating a sunflower-head End
a dirty joke with a punchline and
go silent before Christ

Suddenly a girl with greasy hair and
swollen lymph nodes walks up
to Christ and starts to tickle Him
from heel to pinkie The boy reports
the facial expression of the tickled one

Not knowing why I join them and
together we tickle the frozen God
this way and that We pause a bit and
decide to continue until
something changes

We wait without speaking to
each other We listen

I wait
I listen

In Three Sentences

You believe so that you may kill the
doubt within you.

I doubt so that I may kindle the
faith within me.

You and I are right because the end
has no *raison d'être?*

The Template

Truly, they belong together:
though they may hide their resemblance,
their outcome is the sum
of missed opportunities.

* * *

Everything happens quickly.
Depending on the price,
season, holiday, desire
and a few more random things.

Washing, clothing, wood
choices and other possibilities.
Sometimes there's nothing to wash and wear.
We are in transit.

* * *

Until now I imagined
that everything has its limits.
From now on what passes
human understanding fits
within the limits of good or bad
taste.

Someone like this happened once.
Once in a while someone like this happens.
Someday someone like this will happen.
Even a body as old as the world
also does something in life,
ends its life.

Though hungry for the truth
they nurture hope. Still,
most of the time everyone
dies the same way.
Supine and
sobbing.

* * *

I drink your alcohol, your coffee,
and I take a shower in your tub.
Things happen down the road
that I know nothing about
what is there to say except that
I'm trying to grow
into you.

People You Know

must have died, since you honour within yourself their
updated nonsense. *My guy friend travels the red trail across*
mountains and seas, and my girl friend forcefully attacks the columns
of Noah's Ark, you announce. One day you will sail away unanointed,
and a host of organisms will quietly colonize you. Until recently
I watched the wise mechanisms that push you into the
arms of others, into the grimaces of co-dependency,
the ethics of weighty matters of a good and honest life.
Evidently, life impresses: extreme conditions, which
I have never known, a shot cancelling all heresies.

I don't know how I could help you. Maybe I'll talk
about myself. A case without history. Simply put, nothing
ever happened to me. Everything happened outside of me.
I heard some calls, somewhere in the distance someone
mobilized my dreams. A vortex of intentions
pleas and curses. In the end, I gave up the journey.
Since then, no paragraph applies to me.
Things just go on without my participation. Only
in moments of sheer doubt do I entertain hope and
you.

The North Sea

after Tomas Tranströmer

I.

The philanthropy of waves implies some kind of consent you know nothing about.
It seems that for you, to be taken from this world means a disgrace of appearances,
the irrevocable defeat of future projects, the end of the benefit of doubt
you bestow upon petitioners like yourself. A little moderation, please.
I wouldn't put that much emphasis on it. Nor on anything else.
Your way of killing the sea should remind you of the years you spent in
the swiftness of change, between expectant sin and after-penance.
And the time in-between, which you filled with all kinds of local diagnoses,
convoluted excuses and the reopening of old prejudices.
Of course, the question of characterology is not to be discounted here.
There is certainly a climate of understatement that swallows the greatest part
of your life, the dreams that are yours alone and that allow you
a peaceful sleep of routine dreaming, which occurs every night
for no special reason, considering what we know about dreams today.
But you'd rather await something out of this world, something reeling,
like, say, the grain of poetry hidden in every illiterate being.
Little one, your dilemmas cause me serious trouble.
Meanwhile, watch the sea, it has a happy ending.

II.

On that day the waves refused to obey. We walked on the water.
Everything started to fall into place. We grew certain that our suspicions
were just a kind of metalanguage that led us astray of the proper
understanding of things. It was the day of return to the heart of the script.
The fakery of sunrises and sunsets turned out to be trivial.
We pawned the light, and love went under the hammer.
We rolled up our display of decorum in a blanket, buried death in the sand.
We managed to forget and everyone went back to their problems.
Like you, I think the time for solid realistic prose has come.
We all have similar expectations, especially now when there's so much talk
of returning to basic spiritual dilemmas and reflecting on man's needs
in the age of raging illusions about authentic salvation.
I think that nothing prevents you from trying again.
The risk of resurrection cannot be a warning to us.
So, since it is decided, let it be, my little one.
Come out of the water and I'll write to the typesetter.
He'll put his initials.
You'll put a cross.

In Broad Daylight

seen through the bubble of a spirit level the horizon
once and for all loses its power to encircle
tiptoeing makes your bones grow quiet and painless

I can be absolutely convinced that in broad daylight
with an overcast sky everything repeats itself
and that the blanket wrapped around your legs is upright

the light passes between verses not written
for me but for you alone surely it has been said
that nothing follows even though it converts

Transitions

so this is already the march the exit
straight ahead behind the walker
the pistachio-delinquent says dada
the shadows under the metal sconce reply
nothing can be bright any longer
all must unite into a vast darkness
she loves the coming of daybreak
without her the days are unloved

What Next

the burning will to possess an object
ball thistle morsels hereby
organizes the subject's adventures
delineates their moving horizon
when nothing understands us no one
proposes another meaning
only a spittle of words
except for tongue ball thistle
no one gets it insists on it
or has it any longer

Sleepy Prewar

It seems that I called it Yidkovo, Dad.
It did happen.

Like every day I'm waiting for you to wake up
I'll utter the greetings you know so well,
then, in the blink of an eye, the ritual will begin,
step by step into time, into the promptness
of hours, with a small pause, when suddenly around noon
the source of factual eternities will shine beyond sheet metal
and black shingles, beyond the smoke of burning tar,
a mighty lifting of darkness, smoke tearing
through our rough cloud ceiling, for they are
yours, look closely, this image will draw you close,
it will accompany you like a permanent wall
and I will hear the first screams.

Florida

A familiar face from the antipodes scans the lobby,
greets people with a managerial smile,

she has visited continents, anarchies and orientations,
trod the fitness trail of bitterness,

it didn't have to be like this, wrong plan, supplies and skills,
but you can spot her old features, forever hot

and permanently possessed, when boredom
rustles like an anecdote, *lately things aren't great,*

the heavy wallpaper bursts in the sun of narrowing horizons,
happiness peeks through the cracks, there's someone to open up to,

they searched for someone with a tongue,
this, too, brought me here.

This Rather Than That

Everything resembles itself and barely
hangs on to this perpetual defensive state.
A special effect for non-believers?
And only one by one can we chance the
once and for all, but for the time being

all of us are meaningless to language.

Of Course

He remembers startled birds squealing, stiffness, blood.
Old objects in a new decor. Of course.
Also people. Thanks to whom one can die
of laughter. Without them too.
What will he believe on his own time? Of course,
he doesn't know how he got here, but he knows how to get out.
At least that's what he says. In moments
of happiness.

Skills

He doesn't know what he loses and misses.
He doesn't even know what hit him.
Teach him about himself anew,
repeat yourself. Test his
level of self-knowledge.

It is so: he can cry
in the hotel at dawn,
bicker during a banquet and
take leave of you at the train station.
Among other skills he would list

the ability to turn his mind back to
the times when everything seemed
fabulously simple, like the graph
line
of an electroencephalogram.

Boundaries

Did she let it slip, does she believe it?
All the same it moves him
in ways he cannot afford
because like a frozen mannequin
he must hold the line and not react
to the taunts of life.

Yes, he remembers.
On the back seat of the bus,
in uncomfortable positions,
on levitating legs, dazed,
they had crossed the border,
staring at the customs officers' mugs.

They had nothing to declare
but everything to save,
for though he had buried their rubble,
the scent of her arms and the
taste of one tear seized his throat and
let him drown his guilt in

the cesspit of his insignificance.
He is dirty, as you say,

whence comes his fear? He is difficult
like forgiveness? Is he your
creation confined
by a sick mind?

The Attempt

It looks like he's not ready for
penitence through renunciation.
Always this close. Yet his old self.
He still prevails owing to
positioning her in contexts
that matter in any given sentence.
Still, something seems to have shifted.

There was a moment
when she hated as much as he did.
Unidentifiable by their bodies, they
were pure fury ruining the tenderness
they had previously courted
with the greatest of care by
holding hands.

More such occurrences,
and he'll think some big shot cares
about him on account of his approach
to things best forgotten
if one is serious about
the next attempt to overcome
pain and ridicule.

A List of Essential Practices

—care, caresses and such favourite practices should not suggest any particular interest in the situation at hand.

—we maintain top composure in the moments when we handle private assets, intimate correspondence and so-called personal belongings, access to which is limited by the degree of closeness, family ties or the conventional spectacle of relationships determined by the time spent together.

—outside the execution site, we engage in idle chitchat, especially about everyday troubles, inconveniences and assorted worries, to which we now grant primary status. For example, we are excessively interested in the pet-care system.

—relieving tension and overcoming shame will ensure a common memory of important recent events concerning all who gathered at the place of execution.

—we avoid tears at the place of execution, trying to adopt a fully automated behaviour, ignoring unpleasant impressions and speculative observations.

—we won't refuse a small snack, we won't shy away from a short walk around the neighbourhood, we may offer to help resolve technical matters for which there might be no time later.

—we look for hope in the smallest episodes and movements of the object of punishment, this allows us to dull new opportunities and to embrace possibilities that would ease future struggles.

31

—although we believe in what is not here, we find no words of understanding for a different form of being.

—we practice till we drop.

PART II

Crematoria I

Two into one-and-a-half into a half
There is no other
Dimension

Spittoon

Filled to the brim
Bursting its banks
Showing yesterday's fare
Is consumed

Bathing

Sponge and washcloth
Again and again
Precisely and calmly
Amidst chaos

Patience

Again he calls out

Yet it was explained
Repeated many times
How much can one ask

After (Confessional Poetry)

Piss and bile
The body doesn't care

Discard all your clothes
Return them before, so they won't hang
Afterwards by themselves as a pretext
For who knows what
Questions

Or complaints
There should be nothing
For anyone to raise afterwards

Meanwhile

Curtains drawn
To half-darkness to see above
The windowsill what's going on today
At the Crematoria

What will be missing beside
The sun except for the ashes
Meanwhile it only looks
like a good day

Impersonal

Hygienic pads
Pads of hope

Travellers

Landing in the room
A television
A transistor
A trans

Philately

As in an old stamp album
Cancer upon cancer

Results

Stored meanings
Data
In the folds of time

Columns of dreams
The colour of days
Until the last one

Painting and Imaging

Something's up
Rollers and primers
Get started on the wall
In anger and sadness

But there's no point
A last renovation
A last car
A last effort

For believers
It is good to know
The dryness of cracked lips
And of crumbling crevices

Straight down to the bottom
Of a heart that is not there
Inside the image of a world
Of inner images

What's to hide without them
Layer upon layer
What will be shall emerge
And what must be worse than nothing

Changes

News comes from outside
About things worsening

In paradise
If ever it was

Other than disguised
Palliative fiction

Touching those within reach
Validated by perfection

Becoming anyone's truth
Smoothed to anyone's taste

No longer harmful
Relief comes from loss

You can burn down the house
Before being thrown out

The Numismatist

Heads
Tails
Same outcome

How will you spend
Your homeopathic treasure
After blowing everything
On opiates

Pretend
Lest you howl

Accidental Hope

It's no one's fault
It depends
Which way you look
And at which sky
The one showering
A storm
Of questions

Upon the head resting on a block
The same
Upon which yesterday still
Everything depended
On chance today it depends on
Whether the rot will shrink
Tomorrow if at all

On Your Way Out

Plant a white flag
On the Crematoria

PART III

[The Generous Street of Souvenirs]

The generous street of souvenirs leads to the top of blooming
excavations. A planted flag waves, cheering the new techno-
logies of resurrection developed by your retiree—the ghost
of invention and innovation locked in a cubbyhole for revolut-
ionaries. Other characters worth mentioning are a good-news
pastor, a perpetual protester, and you, the recipient. We mould you
in the shape of a moat and organize exhibitions of ideas. In
memory and honour of those who first strummed humorous strings
of bloated light. In the age of darkness, you looked excess-
ively sharp. Unlike now when the only thing at your dis-
posal is tinder, which is not worth using, since
complete knowledge of the nature of objects has been achieved,
whereas beyond it the sphere of inarticulate contro-
versies comes down to a liking for lexical excesses.

March Report

Bloom and decay characterized all the processes that
I saw. I have nothing to add here. Everything co-
responded in conservative harmony, except the
funeral processions and musical hits of despair, since
they died en route, in a pit of secular soil, and so I saw
them quite differently. They looked motivated, ready to growl
about their discoveries, to howl about hopeful nightmares and
fearful elation. I might have thought of something, but they
didn't care about me. They didn't mention me in their truth
decrees, even if they might have racked their brains. *Did they hold
the key?* By this, did they lose the chance to valorize
their own mistakes, to learn a language in which they would perfect-
ly grasp what is not here? Even if they are
right, the sky today is ideally pure.

Docklands

Finally, a bridge materialized before their eyes. Drawn
by the force of attraction, they crossed over to opulent lights.
      They had left the memory of details in a faraway home, full of
minor understatements the size of matching agonies
suffered by Sunday tourists, landlords of
      a rebellious imagination, or unsuspecting
laymen finding truth in the caves of their own intuition.
Later they changed their plans, but something went wrong. Returning to
      the docks plunged in darkness might be viewed by the uninitiated
as a case of ordinary cold feet, case of midlife wuss or some
common pragmatism before the judgements of fate that we entrust
      to the discretion of a ridiculous accident, new editions of clever
logorrhoea or a vulgar overdose, the missed chance for a life
blooming in the blink of an eye on the most interesting channels. Meanwhile
      they meant not to watch anything from a different perspective.
No brochures, postcards or ads. *We don't care about London's monuments.*
Dear ones, is not the only option to work beyond the current of deep emotions,
      the rot of inner suburbs, the stench of escapism?
In an unknown context, in their spare time, outside of business
hours, they strolled across the sea and the river.
      Silently in the name of the language of justifications.

Bare Facts

Coke lumps in the lungs.
A scraped esophagus.
What's left of life trickles
out with my sperm.

Other outcomes?
I won't be ready
for them anyway.
What, and for what?

[Entering the Dwellings of Sad Religions]

Entering the dwellings of sad religions through abandoned
stone villages, occasional rural metropolises, the
raw ridge of pictorial tongue and truly attractive landscapes.
They coined the word: Welcome. Soaring to the sky through
switchbacks, shaken by laughter like plastic rugs, authentically
and obediently lying along a crooked string of sentences—a phalanx
trampling the social contract of village spirits. Now you are treading
this worn-out route, sneaking through the alleys of forlorn gems whose
painted roofs reflect the obstinacy of a monastic portraitist. You
are leaning on the air he breathed. The empty alley, amphitheatre
and the echo of naughtiness—a quadriphonic imitation
reproduced much later, in different circumstances,
in a completely different setting, in quite unexpected realities.
At least note the cracks in the facades, the gaps in the text, the general
nothingness of life's ventures.

Depth

Of course there is something else to discover.
He sinks in his blood and lymph and all the rest,
just to discover his wreckage,
full of priceless material much sought after
by modern medicine. Everything is precious and
surely could be used if it weren't for one's
attachment to it and the fear of parting with oneself.

Give yourself to him, sweetheart. Give him your hand,
even if you are lying with your back turned and
looking at some old furniture that once
represented someone's world, the concealed treasures
of a green cutlery box, a row
of medals, a birth certificate and a funeral photo.
Now they are caught in a vortex

of renovation, reuse and
loving care, as if they could
double in value just because
they say goodbye to us when,
back-to-back, we sink to the bottom
of our bodies that for a time will be
common property.

Outside the Window

Wet dawn Rain tangles in the vines of the lightning rods
that hang along the edges of buildings In the parking lot
a Beetle is swaddled in a black cover except for
its bumpers that are freezing

Despite warm milk with honey and a thick tracksuit you are
freezing Why did you clean the furniture with denatured alcohol
yesterday now it shines with cold In this room no
God will want to nest anymore

Somehow everything disinfected itself as if
for a surgery that merely confirms there is
nothing left to cut close and save

Am I still allowed to use the telephone?

You dial a number that used to be a real number Silence
You only hear your hard stubble against the receiver

All around the scratching of nothingness gets louder

* * *

Since you must be thinking, think
the same thing in the same way.
Do we find a reason for ourselves right away?
Does this ride have a destination?

We apprentice with the blind. I don't believe
my eyes when I look
over my shoulder. I've arrived.
Is this not the time and place for it?

The City

The city hangs on wires while the dogs wake up. The charred folders
of a colourful bliss fit effortlessly in the hands of a child who's
come from the suburbs. There are other eyes in those eyes,
the multiplied eyes of a little admiral who leads a wooden
fleet of bodies. The dry dock of the royal harbour is covered with duckweed
that reflects the neutral sky. The temple of dawn stands opposite
the glass district, silent in the language of a monotonous melody nobody hums.
No one comes forward in my name, nothing may happen
with my participation. Hence the city's army lies in wait at the corners, a scout
crouches inside a shipping container and looks at my window. I've been in his sights
since I turned on the light. The fumes over the city glow like a wheel
under which rises another kind of sun. The admiral of the one-man city
greets the aura with folded hands. The morning newspapers are as empty as the blaze.

From Afar

They had a good time.
They looked drunk
with happiness. Of course. Delicious
ribs, sauce and potatoes. Afterwards
the three of them stayed
in the dining car, laughing their
heads off. Voluble and piqued.
Deaf to the world of
bigger problems, to which
they were presently returning,
evading their final destinations
without a hitch.
It lasted a little longer before it all
vanished, and in place of people
there appeared objects.
Late into the night he hugged
end tables, shelves and lamps,
checking dead objects' supremacy
over what is still alive
from afar.

False Bottom

It is hard to take a stand on what's happening,
hence being distracted we dare to opine.
With great determination Mrs Kraus stands
by her truth. I can't get over it, she says.
She has been in good health all her life, she says.
She speaks therefore she does not think? Does she think what she says?

Everything requires a supplement to make it
happen. A named thing no longer threatens, remember?
Life fulfilled her worst forebodings
from the moment she started enjoying them.
When you realize that it is too late,
do you give yourself time to think?

A basket full of her lingerie stands next to a bed
full of sheets. The refrigerator is full of empty shelves.
The mini bar is full.
I place a full glass on the table, fill another and
work keeps my hands
full.

From a Diary

Charity appeared at the beginning, actually. We had
so many glitches and defects, and yet our permanent condition
didn't burden or wrong anyone in this situation, which
was simply a brazen interference in the intimacy of matters
already lost that we happened to face. Respect and
gravitas, a brief reverie and wonder, were mere formalities
that we performed the day we abandoned the world of deliberate
hope and joined no one. We remember the time when eyes
went dark and libraries burned, when the seas parted as the leader spoke
between book covers. As we leave, it is worth mentioning that there are many
uses for us, as per the literature on the subject. Sacrifice is a good deed.

Rose

An ill-fitting name for the owner of
such a pale face. Sorry, he didn't mean it.
He just wanted to say that your eyes
match the colour of your sweater, that's it.
That you are put together unusually.
Usually, you are not available to him. How is it
usually? Are they able to organize for themselves
some routine, in the sense he heard
repeatedly, that it is the be-all and end-all.
What did he despise and desire? Fuck knows.
They are condemned to reality, with a hint that they are not.

Particulars and Ideas

Although it quotes itself and
is self-explanatory
the body

in fact clearly
refuses to be switched off
for anything in the world.

So

As repeatedly before, so it is
this time. Giggles and grimaces,
pities worthy of a resolution,
waking hours, hunger and mineral water.
And suddenly a refreshing chill
dreamed of by anyone in
love. But that's not all.
The fun begins the moment
one becomes indifferent.
To be indifferent is to live.

Finally

After everything, he surfs empty channels.
He doesn't speak into the receiver, or he says
anything, any which way, just to be done. It is
high time. Bathrobe, teeth, pillows, exhale.
Three positions. Right side, left side, supine. Finally.
The day isn't used to this. It's got the wrong
addressee.

[A Merciful Amnesia Manages Current Affairs]

A merciful amnesia manages current affairs, the future
is not our business. Don't be afraid, don't bother. Blind sirens
camp on the militarized bluff, a surplus garrison scurries
into the water as if torpedoed, while you are
searching for revelation in columns of treacherous blue.
A night of shooting stars illuminates the panopticon's never-seen
flat surfaces. When you look at them the constellation above you
is enough, and also the satisfaction to be visible in a periscope
as an extraterrestrial body turned into a salt figurine. Just below
the surface of the sand lurks the trickster moment when
ephemeral waves take away the rest of the beached units.
Mishmashed biographies sparkle like fish on a grill.
You can also find trade-union badges, an assortment of
factual knowledge, and a corner with suitable esoterica. For good
measure, you will visit the seal sanctuary at feeding time, when
the pups hop spryly on the scales to the unanimous applause
of the ghost colony. *Exit.*

First Impression

Concrete sarcophagi, dream paradise for a troubled teen
reliving his sorrows in a wonderful mood.
Meanwhile, I see crystal-clear perspectives, a twirling sky,
heated oxygen that turns those revelations to ash, no matter what.
What have we got here? A shabby biomass stretched on poles,
thickets of light, a fjord vanishing in the distance, full of depth, as
this land that yields to death. This doesn't mean anything,
doesn't help negate anything, but relieves you
of having to ponder a greater dilemma, be it
the situation of nits in the proverbial bed, or deities that
burst under the fingernails of hands folded in too-ardent
prayers. Right now there's nothing to worry about, just
admiration: a skip, a schooner, a smile.

* * *

Yes, I'm testing viewpoints. To see you,
wrongheaded, in front of the mirror looking
into my eyes. Your lame smile, in the blue light,
somehow comments on matters further to be
determined by a stranger, a sardonic defeatist,
time spent fighting the hospital's juncture and corrupt
outreach. As you close the door behind you, imagine
that I'm already there waiting for some good news.

April Fools' Day

Is it good for some matters to have been weighed
and for our influence to end there?

To have peace is to keep pretending that
everything is headed in the right direction, I tell you.

Everything I don't touch touches me.
Whatever I would not do, I always do.

How to conceive that a conceived body
is already run-down and earmarked?

Of the many jokes I was the butt of,
this one brought me to tears:

I open my eyes at dawn and
lose my mind from the get-go.

Belief System

Report on anything, because what happens to you may
remind others of what to remember, yet nothing kills
more than shared experiences.

I knew it then, and now we are splitting up
in the same direction and I can see
that we haven't met before because
you are asking me what's up.

Apparently, I never listened to what I was saying.
In the future, I promise to pay a little more attention
to myself, since you no longer make me wait for you.

A Way of Life

Wrapped in tissue I found a curl and a baby tooth.
Final beginnings so carefully preserved.
A little nothing. To kill time,
between God and truth.

Settling Scores

under the sand under the grains of sand fuzzy
finger drawings travel someone's breviaries
phantasmagories doodles to which you give shape
seated without a care in the world scattering your bucket

as if everything were counted in the name of changing
someone else into some non-existent thing that will
uneasily emerge years later from waves
seized by trembling arms and grabby hands

pure bitterness overflows precisely in your happy moment
away from the source but within reach of the watchful gaze that
wants to believe that the end may be slower or different

but since it can't make up its mind it looks away
counts the grains until the toenail clipper can't go any further
from there the sentences will flow and the right speech

A New Novel

Nothing came out of the experiments,
industrial salt uncovered what was
to uncover, some powderized faeces,
butts from last year's libation, footprints
running after the first morning buses,
long-lost development blueprints
return now in the sun of new possibilities,
the first investors poke sticks around the well,
talk up a bright future to someone
who will have to start chasing after it,
obtain funds, lose his fears, leave
his pad, bedbug hovel, hopeless corner,
that, after all, was enough, but he craved a boost,
yielded to the vision of a better tomorrow,
without himself, in another world, so he promised,
I'll get something too, something humming in the mud,
keep kicking yourself to the end of the world, man.

The Speaker

for Mariusz

Satisfying arguments for all eternity, your inner
speaker draws them out into the daylight. Future and past
controversies no longer count. He leads you to the pilloried window
where a commando unit of women appears, strapped in company
uniforms, bedraggled by resignation to the overgrown fence
of an absentee landowner. They start to suck the air,
with newsmonger tongues and bowed heads that pay tribute to
the thistles. Patient as a budding freak, they pelt you with earth when
you tell them to get moving and go home. There is no history. No way
do they believe in anything. Always the same, first thing in the morning.

Translators' Afterword

In a recent article published in *World Literature Today*,* Krzysztof Siwczyk speculated that the future of Polish literature belonged to the essay, calling it 'a defective, discontinuous, highly mysterious literary genre'. Additionally, Siwczyk praised the capaciousness of the form, where both 'the idioms of one's own language and a somewhat narcissistic eloquence' could not only coexist but also reinforce each other. That these words came from one of Poland's most innovative poets might surprise some, but only until we remember the adage according to which all criticism is autobiographical. Was, then, Siwczyk writing about himself and the direction his writing might take? It would seem so, as he's been increasingly turning his artistic and intellectual attention towards essay writing over the last several years, but it's equally true that what he appreciates about the essay is also what makes his poetry exhilarating.

Siwczyk, who was born in 1977 and has lived most of his life in the Silesian city Gliwice, became the latest wunderkind of the Polish poetry scene when he published his debut volume, *Dzikie dzieci* (Wild Kids), in 1995. Edgy and unsentimental in its portrayals of the eponymous youth of Siwczyk's

* Krzysztof Siwczyk, 'After the Transitions' (Alice-Catherine Carls trans.), *World Literature Today* 97(3) (2023): 62–5. Available at: https://bit.ly/3QD1dNX [last accessed on 10 May 2024]

surroundings against the backdrop of Poland lurching from communism to capitalism, the poems also offered a mix of urban impressionism and *je ne sais quoi* stemming from the speaker's awareness of being at the cusp of something bigger than himself. 'I wait / I listen,' we read at the conclusion of the title poem, but it didn't take long for the poet to make his next move.

Having penned a de facto youth manifesto in *Dzikie dzieci*, Siwczyk could've settled into the role of a chronicler of urban malaise and adolescent trials and tribulations; instead, he went deep, as it were, into language, taking to heart the notion that language speaks through us and not the other way around. The fact that this turn occurred after Polish poets had internalized Frank O'Hara and John Ashbery is an important touchstone, but to dwell on Siwczyk's predecessors and models, someone like Andrzej Sosnowski, for example, would be doing him a disservice, because Siwczyk has always been a trenchant poet, unafraid to break taboos and call out established figures. After all, a poet-essayist writes not only about what he sees but also what he feels and thinks, and, even more importantly, about what is outside the realm of the known—in an attempt to express or articulate the ineffable.

As a poet whose craft is characterized by a certain dynamism, in many a poem Siwczyk careens down the page at great speeds, taking us on a zany ride, relying on key moments—a turn of phrase or an idea—which he calls 'illuminations', to convey a larger meaning. As in calligraphy, a circuitous process of connecting semantic meaning and memories accompanies the choreography of thought and verse. In the process, words and images are teased to the surface in rapid, terse and precise bursts. For example, in one poem, Siwczyk writes, 'The generous street of souvenirs leads to the top of blooming / excavations' (p. 53 in this volume), as he unravels something palpable and poignant. Siwczyk's close examination of the dichotomy between the language we speak and our inability to express or communicate is equally troubling and nourishing.

Siwczyk's unceasing determination not only to fathom our world but also to continually prod our sense of identity and belonging has led him to change course multiple times. After several volumes of poems with his trademark expansive lines and logorrhoea, along with the early works marked by narrative energy, he recently released a trilogy of poems on illness and grief—some of these appear in Part II of this volume. These clipped and understated poems, from the collection *Krematoria I, II, III* (2021–2022), evoke the Holocaust and the ability of human beings to bear witness of death and tragedy.

If in the earlier volumes, the reader could sense uncertainty and transience vis-à-vis the milieu, they have now become the proverbial sum of their parts both physical and imaginary—as can be read in 'Results' (p. 44): 'Columns of dreams / The colour of days'. Desperate to ease the suffering of a loved one, the speaker in *Krematoria* is despondent, ascribing everything to blind chance (for example, in 'The Numismatist', p. 47: 'Heads / Tails / Same outcome'), yet the gesture of unfurling a white flag at the hospital connotes, paradoxically, a way out and a regained sense of purpose.

A volume of selected poems translated from a minor language, such as Polish, raises questions about what's included and what's omitted. Comparisons and considerations of literary lineage inevitably arise in such contexts. This is particularly evident in books that introduce new Polish poets to a global readership, given the widespread popularity and acclaim of stalwarts such as Czesław Miłosz, Wisława Szymborska or Adam Zagajewski. However, it is worth noting that Krzysztof Siwczyk has studied his compatriots closely—their success, indeed, presents a welcome challenge—while forging his own path in contemporary world literature.

In other words, he is deeply aware of the bardic role that Poland, owing to its history, has placed upon its poets, while infusing his idiolect with the readings gleaned from world literature. The poet's desire not to be pinned down in terms of form, style or subject, is also why we have avoided specific markers that would signal a sense of chronology to the readers. This decision also reflects our belief that selected poems in translation should remain untethered from tradition constraints or contextual limitations and instead be read as a complete volume. The sixty-four poems in *A Calligraphy of Days* convey our reading of the poet, and represent a sincere attempt to channel the fascinating world of Krzysztof Siwczyk's wide-ranging and variegated poetry in a single, succinct volume.

Translators' Acknowledgements

For their suggestions, love and support of this work, the translators would like to thank Daniel Simon and Cecilia Woloch (*The Atlanta Review*).

Many thanks to Krzysztof Siwczyk for his trust and patience.

Lots of gratitude to the amazing team at Seagull Books.